MADSTONES

MADSTONES

COREY MESLER

BLAZEVOX[BOOKS]
Buffalo, New York

Madstones
by Corey Mesler
Copyright © 2018

Published by BlazeVOX [books]

All rights reserved. No part of this book may be reproduced without the publisher's written permission, except for brief quotations in reviews.

Printed in the United States of America

Interior design and typesetting by Geoffrey Gatza
Cover Art: "Madstones" by Amanda Bearden

First Edition
ISBN: 978-1-60964-323-2
Library of Congress Control Number: 2018951448

BlazeVOX [books]
131 Euclid Ave
Kenmore, NY 14217
Editor@blazevox.org

publisher of weird little books

BlazeVOX [books]

blazevox.org

21 20 19 18 17 16 15 14 13 12 01 02 03 04 05 06 07 08 09 10

BlazeVOX

Table of Contents

A is Easy 11
Dapping for Meaning 12
Bitter my tongue 13
After the Vandals Sacked Rome 14
Just a Little 15
And Sleep 16
I think of you in poems 17
In Double Indemnity 18
Woodpecker 19
Father, Son 20
Eucalyptus, I Calyptus, We all Calyptus 21
In attitudes of love 22
A murmuration of starlings 23
A troubling of goldfish 24
Jim at the Window 25
Madstones 26
Kool like Klaus Kinski 27
I Never Saw my Father Drunk 28
Young and Hot 29
The Best Cowboy 30
A barefoot woman 31
Night Voyage 32
Portrait 33
She drank, was wild 34
Here 35
Dark Things 36
Bosch 37
Inauguration Day 2017 38
Starting with my Penis 39
Gloria Grahame Grays 40
In Jackson, Mississippi 41
Song 42
Home in the City 43

Limning the Dream	44
Distortion	45
And the Snow Covered Everything	46
Chekhov	47
Inside Again	48
Chiasmatype	49
The Edge of You	50
The Dog's Song	51
Gathering, Disruption	52
The Ghost-Me	53
Ophelia	54
Ophelia 2	55
Four Poems	56
Asterisk	57
Third Poem	58
Meridiem	59
Thirteen Years	60
The World's Fattest Man	61
Mensuration	62
My World and Welcome to It	63
The Dark Clock	64
The Recovery	65
Sneak Thief	66
In my Library	67
Snowlight	68
Torn	69
LSD	70
I can't fix it either	71
The Word would be Go	72
Seeing the Pill Clearly	73
I Go Out, I Expect Things	74
Once the Poem Ran like a Dream	75
I Have Terrible Mornings	76
Dorothy Parker	77
And—	78
Beast	80
O for a Muse of Fire	81
We've Got Life	82

Bruegel	83
Huldre Vigilate	84
Ministration	85
The Wolf Again	86
Ring-a-Lievio	88
The Medicine Bottle	89
The Idea	90
I used to be a king	91
Dog	92
Let's Do This	93
Meditation on a Thurible	94
My bird	95
Little One	96
CONTRANYMS	97
A.M.	100

MADSTONES

"Are there not stones in heaven/But what serve for the thunder?"
--William Shakespeare

"I am glad we live in a thingy world."
--Iris Murdoch

*"Now Helicon must pour streams in me,
Urania with her choirs assist me here,
to put in verse things hardly thinkable."*
--Dante

For my Cheryl and for wee Sylvi

A is Easy

A is easy,
a gate,
a way in,
even
for the most
ill-prepared.
A is the
letter
I sent you
asking
you to come back.
Return
to A,
I think I said.
The gate
is always open.

Dapping for Meaning

I took my fishing rod down to
the stream of consciousness
and tried to hook a story
about love and lust and that feeling
of incomprehensible bliss that
only exists in the rushing, toppling
waters of the stream of consciousness
on whose banks I sat for years
thinking about what if, only what if.

Bitter my tongue

The heart is heavy
as the ironmonger's
store. The light out-
side stays outside.
I wake to the air of
the cardinal, a scrape
of song. Day passes to
night. When it is
time I will lie down
again and think of you.
You must be as you
were, distant, clean, &
corrupt as a collapsed star.

After the Vandals Sacked Rome

Mischief! cried one man on horseback,
his tunic stained with either paint
or blood. They must be drunk,
said the priest, watching as his altar
was adorned with a Nash Rambler
grill. One woman, shirtless, reveler
or victim, kept shouting obscene slogans
in Latin, while her boyfriend decorated
the Coliseum walls with phony gang tags.
After the Vandals sacked Rome they
rode slowly home, their horses still wearing
absurdities: a nightgown, a toilet seat,
the golden crown of a Nobleman. Some
stayed behind for the wine and outdoor
copulation. Some later became Romans them-
selves. Most went home to a life too ordinary.
Everything seemed pale and lackluster. Oh, for
the days of pillage! they cried over their
beer. Had someone known to tell them that
their very names would become synonymous
with recklessness and abandonment it
probably would not have helped. The post-coital
blues are like a tapeworm, sickly and nearly eternal.

Just a Little

> *"Dead love stories are what make us."*
> *--Kevin Barry*

There was the afternoon
in the brackish pool.
There was the diner—
healthy food, tasteless
in your dazzle. There
was the bookcase, an
excuse to lean together.
And there was the first
naked moment and
the soft incantation:
you can put it in just a little.

And Sleep

I tear the pages from the almanac and
fear the weather on every page.
And sleep.
I count the children as they pass through
the door, meticulously, with love and terror.
And sleep.
I make what I can from what I am given, small
doses, some not quite powerful enough.
And sleep.
I talk to you about the things which seemingly
make us intimates.
And sleep.
And I sleep and dream of everything I could not
do, the things which should have come
naturally, like medicine, or the rules,
and I am lost, lost, wanting only to hold you one
more time on the way down,
to love you as hard as I ever loved you and then
to lie down at last, near you again, and sleep, sleep.

I think of you in poems

I think of you in poems.
It is not the only time.
Some days are full of blather
and architecture and cost.
Sometimes I write to find out
if I can write. These are things
I would say to you if I loved
you. This is that cracked song.

In Double Indemnity

"How could I know that murder can smell as sweet as honeysuckle?"

In Double Indemnity
much is made
of Barbara Stanwyck's
anklet. It's a grace note
in the grey
web of story. Fred
McMurray is one gone
motherfucker, giving up
his freedom, his heart, and
eventually everything
to the *idea* of Stanwyck's
love. No one's heart is
engaged and no one's heart
is broken. Bring it back
to that anklet. It shines
as every other light
is extinguished;
darkness, sepulchral darkness,
descends, and now
the film closes its steady eye.

Woodpecker

My wife hears the woodpecker's
maraca and is
drawn outside
into the icy air.
Later she shows me a photograph
of the woodpecker,
frozen, still, soundless and blurred.

Father, Son

In five years you would have been
one hundred, but Father,
you barely made eighty. I
don't know about souls, but
if you could return, there is much
still to discuss. I need you
corporeal. I need the strength of your
hands and the calm of your stillness.
I am not strong or still. I am
fretful and loud sometimes, which
you never were. I brood and
I am small. Father, in five years
you will be one hundred and, if
I make it on this plane, I will be
sixty-seven. My son will be older, too,
and sometimes I see you in him. In his
quiet grace and his strength and his
loyalty. Father, son, the tree grows upward
and in the dark its branches look like a
ladder. In the morning there is only bird
song, and light, and I am looking, looking up.

Eucalyptus, I Calyptus, We all Calyptus

My friend Ward is a nature poet.
He knows bipinnate vs. odd-
pinnate; he knows the
trails of Nowhere. I am the
man left behind
in the zinc tub, electrodes
attached to his trochee.
I want to write about the bird on
my porch, the one in the
tails and spats. I can only hum.
I can only call him 'small
brown thing.' But, listen, after
dark, when nature drowses, I
am in the lab studying. I want
an artificial woman who
will love me the way some
of you love your houseplants.
A human being so divine
it's as if she is made of no-
thing extant. She would be a god,
and I a godmaker, eternal as a seep.

In attitudes of love

In attitudes of love
you gave and I shook
like a pillar. In
attitudes of love we
talked some more about
the new assassinations
and the country that was
ours when we were we.
In attitudes of love
you undressed and I kissed
the long, perfumed line
of you, supine, your ass a
spine's perfect punctuation.
In attitudes of love
I wrote petitions like this,
never knowing you did
not love me, nor that I
would remember how sorry
it seemed I stayed and stayed.

A murmuration of starlings

A murmuration of starlings
at the bird feeder,
and dirt-bathing beneath,
recalls for me,
inexplicably, how I would
place my palm
on your soft, pale stomach,
and feel the universe there,
so young, so
numinous, so full of dying stars.

A troubling of goldfish

"Nature's first green is gold."
--Robert Frost

Last day.
First day.
Do not leave me.

Sky above.
So below.
Stay while there

is still light.
I am a
pilgrim by streams.

I want things
I do not need.
Do not leave me.

The water runs.
The light finds
a troubling of goldfish.

Jim at the Window

Jim couldn't get the window unstuck. She was about to pass; it was Monday. Mondays she wore that blue dress. She had legs. Today he would speak to her. He was going to call from the window. He saw her near. The sun blinded him. Jim, fondly, began to scream.

Madstones

for Linda Heck

The dogs in the woods have all been
blessed. They are no longer
subject to the moon's recalcitrance.
A small girl, no bigger than
a whisper, clad in white, brought out
the stone. I placed it on the table
with the others, underneath the glim
of Dee's ball. Late at night,
while I am seeking the elusive slipstream
of sleep, I can hear the stones.
They are muttering secret names for
maladies I am only now beginning to harvest.

Kool like Klaus Kinski

The milk train was out of milk.
The flea market of fleas.
We gathered on the docks
to sing the songs of resentment.
Ippy said he'd love a woman
with big HGVs, if she spoke
smooth as Deborah Kerr.
I lit my last cigarette on a
streetlight's reflection. Janis
said she was leaving me for
a marsupial. I wanted to say I'll
stay with the boys who know
boy things. I wanted to be the
writer of the group, though no
one read. I wanted to be you,
Jesse James, kool like Klaus Kinski.

I Never Saw my Father Drunk

I never saw my father drunk
yet he drank every
day, 2 to 3 beers in the evening,
bourbon on weekends.
He was a quiet man, un-
assuming, I guess you'd say.
He never talked about the
war, nor did he ever seem
to carp about his life. Perhaps
he was happy. Perhaps it's that
simple. Evenings, with his
drink, he often worked crosswords,
unless Gunsmoke or Mannix was
on. I heard him disagree with my
mother once. The house grew
so still afterward I thought some-
thing had died. The next night
nothing was changed. My father,
steady as a plaster mask,
sipped his bourbon and found the
exact words to complete his puzzle,
words he never felt burdened to share.

Young and Hot

Sometimes the sound
from the other room
was poetry.
We dared each other
to listen. You began
to unbutton your shirt.

The Best Cowboy

I dreamed I was the best cowboy in the
TV set. The blonde with the bassoon
took notes. She was the belle of the
belfry. She spelled my name the way the
angels will write it. I brodied through a
dust storm, wound up drunk and beautiful:
my eyes, my six gun, my improvised demise.

A barefoot woman

"Be the flame, not the moth."
--Giacomo Casanova

A barefoot woman, a
bush budding.

A winding path, a
path.

The saw of wasps in
the eave, the

small brown tit in the
dust. O why has the bare-

foot woman come? To see
me, my friends, to

touch me the way humans do,
and to be touched, extravagantly.

Night Voyage

In the dark
I lost my way.
I could hear
the boatman
calling, his
voice like an
echo of an echo.
How far away
am I? Ahead
I think I see
my father
dead now twelve
years. Is he
guiding me, again,
or is he a dis-
traction, like
waves breaking?
Now all is silent.
My father is gone
if my father
it was. And the sea
is dead calm as if
chiseled from marble.

Portrait

"It is our noticing them that puts things in a room, our growing used to them that takes them away again and clears a space for us."
  --Marcel Proust

Put a man and a woman
in a room. It's the
first time. She's nervous,
younger than he. He
stops to make tea. Put
the tea in matching mugs,
no, it says too much. Put
the woman at ease. The man
only wants to talk. She
reaches for his hand and
maybe he takes it. Stop it
there. Freeze the portrait.
The two hands. The room,
crisp, crackling, the
tea on the sideboard, cooling.
Stop it. There.

She drank, was wild

She drank, was wild-
er than I had
ever been. It frightened
me a bit and
when she rode me and
exhorted me to bite
her distended nipple hard
I faltered. I was a dis-
appointment to her.
I repeat: I was frightened
a bit and when she left
me, seemingly with-
out reason, I howled like
a mewling child
taken, O God too early,
from the tit.

Here

Here I am: bone.

Here is my eye,
paling.

Here is where I
stopped: sleep.

And, here and
here, where

I put my last words.

Dark Things

When I was five,
on 8th Street in Lewiston, NY,
there was a girl
named Sandy, my age, just
down the street.
We played doctor. I was ill.
I thought there was
a blackness following me, some-
thing I could not
make Sandy's mother understand.
I was afraid, like
a five-year-old, of things un-
known. I did not
know they were in my head.
Sandy, wherever you
are now, thank you for lowering
your shorts. And, oh,
those things,
those dark things only I saw,
have followed me and are
with me still, fifty years
later, and a thousand miles away.

Bosch

The vagarious old man, bent like a tree,
crossing against the light in Midtown,
dressed in soiled robes the same hue as his
mottled beard, may be the painter, Bosch.
Someone calls to him and he looks up, his
face catching the red of the falling sun,
his eyes full of devils and torture and delight.

Inauguration Day 2017

On this damned
day of crows and
beetles the sun shrunk
the trees burnt ghouls
the soil dim fen
I am lucky to know
where all the letters are.
I put an I here. I put
u there. It will end
badly. It will end badly.

Starting with my Penis

I want to start with my penis:
the conversation chugs
away on its own track,
once started it moves toward
you, your stomach, flat like
wind over wheat, your thighs,
those shy monsters, your
lips, where sound becomes song
which leads me toward the
gate, your gate with its
partially tidied sashes, its
squeaky hinge; it's not a gate,
it's your mother part, your
midnight where I want to end up,
awake together, in beds blue
like midnight, the oil in the lamps
running low, all the movement
toward the center where I wait
with a poem for you, a bouquet of
inmost desires, in my hand a penis.

Gloria Grahame Grays

Well, you're about as romantic as a pair of handcuffs.
--from The Big Heat

I woke up in a black and white bed.
Gloria Grahame was sleeping
beside me, her hair upon the pillow
like moonlight in a martini.
I couldn't remember how I got there,
a bar, a car, a gunsel with
cheap patter. All I knew was that I
wanted to be far away. I wanted
to be in another state, with my memory
returned, with my head straight
as a razor's edge. I wanted to take
Gloria Grahame away from the
noir life. I wanted her to see what kind
of man I am, or could be, once
moving down another road, in another
story, without shadows, a
life as clean as moonlight in a martini.

In Jackson, Mississippi

I remember you bent over the antique bed
in your house in Jackson, Mississippi.
The bed was white as the inside of an apple.
Your body was an arc of pleasure.
When I entered you it was like
entering rain. You reached around and
held me in place, a touch not unlike love.
I said, you are such a wonderful lover,
and you returned the lob. Days went
by and weeks and months. I divorced a
terrible wife. You found another man to lie
in that bed and watch you ride him
as if he were as solid as a root. I wept be-
cause I was surrounded by loss. I wept
because you were as sexy as a blaze
and I knew, oh, that as much as
twenty years later I would write this poem.

Song

The plum
left on the
counter
became a
prune
and an old
man sang
his dying song
long into the
white lace
of midnight.

Home in the City

The city ticks in me
like a black clock;
not a heart, no,
never a heart. When
the lights come up,
as the evening
spreads its gray web,
I find the street
where I was born. Then
the very house. I
stumble on its steps,
and from deep in
the interior, I hear the
sound of a
stranger waking
from a dream about me.

Limning the Dream

Today I write the poem
that limns the dream,
the one where you were
both lover and daughter,
where you both loved me
and cheated on me.
The past is an open sore.
The past is a classroom
where the tests come
before anyone is ready.
I helped you with your math,
problems that became poems
because poems is all I know.
I helped you pass and
in return you cuckolded me.
You were my last best lover.
You were my daughter
growing older, growing toward
leaving. And I woke
with a heart sore from what
is imagined, from what
dreams dish out like pun-
ishment. I woke thinking of
you, seeing your face here
in the template where my
life goes from past to future
without a stop, without
even a ripple of contentment.
Save us all from content-
ment, my last and best lover.

Distortion

I am quiet now, like
the root, like the
pond. I come to you,
a breeze. You
feel me and I have already
passed on. You
touch your own cheek.
A partial memory
occurs to you, something
slim like a shadow.
Something shallow, and slim.

And the Snow Covered Everything

A universal blanket of white,
we chose to see it as a benison.
It covered our rotting swingset,
our dog dish, the abandoned
tools. It covered our reasons for
staying inside, our recalcitrant
hunger, our memory of why we
came to this, why we saw this as
some kind of conclusion. It
covered our bad feelings, the
pettiness between us, the bitter
perfume of endings. For a day, for
two, we looked out upon our property
and saw only a blank to be filled
in, a field where we could start
over. When the thaw came—and
it came quickly—it was all we
could do to put the blinders back
on before we were denuded ourselves.
We avert our eyes. We don't see
the mudholes, the mire, the rot.
Remember when it snowed? we
say now. Remember when it was
all covered up? Remember the
way the light bounced off it as if
it were a mirror or a sea of glass?
Remember how much we loved,
really deeply loved, the snow?

Chekhov

And so I read Chekhov,
putting in the hours,
following his lead
through the labyrinths of
the human heart.
And so I read Chekhov
and then rested.
I was late coming to him;
he hit me like a swarm.
Something echoed,
and again echoed.
I set the book aside to rest.
The book sat by me
and hummed like a small
engine. Quietly, with
dark clarity, it said my name.

Inside Again

I'm locked inside with myself again.
I cover the mirrors with paintings.
I open the drapes because the doctor
told me to. I open the door but only
wide enough for djinns to enter.
I open my mouth and begin to sing.
I sing the song you taught me, the
one that begins, O terrible human heart!

Chiasmatype

> *noun—genetics:*
> *the process of chiasma formation, which*
> *is the basis for crossing over.*

I want the bridge, the
crossing over. I want
to live where you live.
I want to wake up in a
place where the color
of the sun is the color
I see inside the simplest
poem. I want to speak
into your hair the words
that deliver me from the
wreckage of my attempt
to travel. And when the
day is done I want to
cross over again, to a
country where the leaders
talk like parrots, like
streams running clear,
like the mouths of caves.
I want to cross over with
you, my lily white. And I want
the crossing to be our final act.

The Edge of You

I knew that standing on the
edge of you
was dangerous. It wasn't the
falling in
that was ticklish. It was the
language your
chaotic abyss used to call me,
the secret tongue
that I thought was extinguished.

The Dog's Song

in memory of Fly

I want to sing the way
our dog sings,
notes that pay attention,
notes that hang
in the air like incense.
I want to know her song
and why she waited
until she was old to begin it.
I want to sing the song
that she knows, the one
of approaching quietus.

Gathering, Disruption

(1) Gathering

The swelling comes and
goes. The light fails.

We come from a country
of snow and coal, one
woman says.

Another man all afternoon
watches the door being built
into the strong white wall.

(2) Disruption

One woman
falls among the discarded
garments.

The water leaks into
the vacant corners.

At night
someone comes with a flashlight,
someone plans to leave
while it's still dark.

The Ghost-Me

The ghost-me appeared in my mirror
while I was out buying groceries.
By the time I got back he had taken
my place in the living room.
Now, most nights, we play backgammon
or one of the ancient games.
The ghost-me takes his time with every
move. It is his studied silence
that unnerves me most. His silence,
his ingenuity, his book-smarts.
Yesterday he asked me to move out. I
have nowhere to go. I have no one to
take me in. The ghost-me doesn't
listen to such negativity. He says I
am only as good as I pretend to be.
I hate his homilies, too. The ghost-me has
replaced me now from tip to toe.
He asked me to write this to you, my wife.

Ophelia

I still see her pink ribbons floating,
the water around her bubbling and
conscious of her expanding death. Her
dress rose like water-columns,
her eyes still tender and pleading.
Several small boys gathered
when they dragged her out, when the
police stood around silent and almost
passionate. Several cars parked here
and there, several people stood on the
outer rim of the tragedy and exchanged
sighs. All around, out in the suburbs,
kitchen lights came on, night fell, and
the wind caught in the trees.
Several nights later the water was still,
the bank dry, the imprint of her body gone.

Ophelia 2

In the evening
she liked to play Ophelia
and watch her
dress bloom like death
until it covered her
eyes, made young by this
late desire to leave
her husband, this
life, a royal pain in the ass.

Four Poems

1
Four knights on zebras come
charging over the amethystine hill brandishing
signs advertising four separate whiskeys.

2
Outside of the caretaker's window four children
are throwing apetalous plants onto the derbies
of these gentlemen in the mackintoshes.

3
At noon on the shopping plaza parking
lot a grocery cart collides with a tan wagon.
In the wagon are four polaroids of newborn babies.

4
Outside every house in this neighborhood a
man stands poised to knock. He will wait till
four o'clock. He has four new death certificates.

Asterisk

When she was younger she wore
her hair in a ponytail.
She still keeps the rubber bands on her dresser
where she sits
and drops tears into them
nights.

Third Poem

Sometimes the third poem
matters most,
the one begun to finish
the ink.
Sometimes it rings like a
clarion, calling
in the last metaphors
from the glistening, bright field.

Meridiem

So here we are
moving around in the dark
bumping into things.

Here we are
wishing we were younger
and more vital,
wishing we could take hold
like a good spell of weather.

So here we go
stepping into buckets,
tripping
over toy fences,
spinning around and around,
palms pressed
to our unbelieving eyes,
the sun not even our friend,
not even the wind.

Thirteen Years

Younger, I rolled her around
like a version of dank reverie.
We fit like a fit.
She left me shaking my head
wondering why,
even this long after, thirteen
years, two wives and two kids.

The World's Fattest Man

I was a young sylph. I
was clueless.
I had 50 cents and I
paid to see him.
We were led in a semi-
circle trudge round his
seat. Not three feet
from me, his face
was indifferent, perhaps
masking contempt.
I was shamed. I
knew we were
the freaks; we wanted to
see something worse
than us, more animal,
more meat. I went
home and my mother
had left a cake out on
the counter, multi-
tiered and beautiful,
like a castle, like
fairy tale fare: dark,
mysterious, transformative.

Mensuration

It's not the heat
so much

the escaped strangler told them

it's the humility.

My World and Welcome to It

In one Twilight Zone
a couple find themselves
in a faux world:
faux tree, sawdust squirrel,
empty buildings. Turns
out it's a doll house
and they are prisoners of
a giant child. I did
not need this denouement.
I don't expect the world
to live for me, the
tree to make syrup, the
neighbors to be available
in my solitude. I am free
from the fear of giant
rulers. I am carefree in
this world of hollow props
and inanimate wildlife. On the
way home I kick over a policeman.

The Dark Clock

"There's a man going round taking names."
--Leadbelly

The clock in my heart tells me
it's time to bleed. I have
one good arm but still
desire to box, to cuff the man
I once was. There is
cruelty in the way the flesh dips
toward midnight, a guttering
candle behind the eyes. Yesterday
I took Miranda into the
dark room and undressed her like
a saint. She told me that two
arms were too many, anyway, but
I lost her when the shade was
raised. In the light none of us
are what we want to be. None
of us have lost the memory of a
self that once walked the world with
a panther on a leash. I recite
the prayer I was taught by the
man who said he was my father: Father,
let me be the person you believe I
can be. Let me be the last to understand.

The Recovery

The recovery from
the storm
took weeks,
then minutes.
Soon, it was simple
to ask anyone
for the time,
the right way to
anywhere. Soon, the
city took on the
glow of afterburn.
And we parishioners
walk around
as if we have always
loved the cracked
oak, the
four-way stop, the
cathedral, roofless.

Sneak Thief

It's more a drift than a fall:
the edges of consciousness
begin to canker, life-fear
gets its foot in. I am sitting
on my throne, my children
scattered around me like
myrrh and frankincense. I
start to tremble inside. Hello,
demon master. I thought,
foolish human rodomontade,
I had left you back in the
black, dead days. Imagine
my surprise to see you in
the face of my beautiful
daughter, in the hands of
my assiduous need to write.

In my Library

In my library
there are books about other books.
There are stories
you'd rather not hear.
There are men and women cavorting
through fictional jungles
carrying wild animals under their
coats. There are poems in
obscure languages, languages
that no one uses anymore.
In my library
there are a million reasons to keep
moving on, forgetting
the bad news today, forgetting
just what makes us
fragile and human and communicators.
In my library
there is the last word in prayer, the
one that ends, amen.

Snowlight

To wake
and
without rising
understand
how
white the light
is
and to under-
stand
the reason
for it:
this fresh icing.

Torn

You ask me, during downtime
in our cage, if
I want to go for a walk. I have to
consider carefully.
To agree lends power to
jeopardy, to stay still
means I am target, footless, emasculate.

LSD

We were all out walking our incunabula.
The streets were paved with blandishment.
Star said, let's wait till the calendar changes.
It will happen within us and without us.
We shouldered our bazookas and went in
search of a way out of the melting daylight.
In the end it didn't matter where we ended up.
The journey, Triscuit said, is more important
than the sitcom about the hillbillies.
Come the sunrise we all declothed and made
a circle, attached at the genitalia. It
was Rebirth. It was the beginning of something
mythoclastic, Coyote said. Something that
each of us believed, held dear, regurgitated.
Acid, the acid said, is the way to the way
that is no-way. The road is paved with anima.
We all, you know, shine on, we all said.

I can't fix it either

for Julien Baker

I can't fix it either.
Either the weather
is too something
or the sound diminishes
like walking into a
room and forgetting
whose home it is. I
can't expect it to even
out, even here, among
those I once recognized.

The Word would be Go

We carried with us
all the tools we would need
to undo things from our end.
Those in charge
sent ahead for the word.
The word would be go.
All along the road,
strung like rough stones on
a piece of string,
stood the people from the towns.
The towns were the
first to go. The fragile towns.
When night came
and we had heard nothing,
from front or rear,
we grew restless.
The moon hung above us like
a jaundiced tear.
The night was alive with
our exhalations.
Our breath suspended in the chill
like small clouds,
briefly beautiful and swiftly gone.
The word finally came.
With it our only hopes, yet we
could not move.
Our immobility became a fever.
The tools dangled heavy
in our hands like redundant arms,
superfluous and onerous.
The tools expected things we could
now no longer deliver.

Seeing the Pill Clearly

The light is so right
that I see the pill
clearly,
not for the first time
mind you,
but as if it were placed
in my
palm by unseen hands.
It fairly
shines
and when I touch it
with a
finger it
feels exactly like a pill.
Swallowing it
seems an afterthought,
just something
I did
after I saw the pill so
clearly
on this bright and sensuous
midwinter
morning, here at the end
of a bad year.

I Go Out, I Expect Things

I stood on the road
and expected it all to come to me.
Mea culpa.
When it rains, that's me out there,
face upwards,
drowning in good intentions. You,
who have seen so much,
tell me where this is going. I will
believe just about
anything, except that I've made a
mistake, or that I've tried
too hard to be who you want me to be.

Once the Poem Ran like a Dream

I get under the poem to see if the rattling
is coming from its chassis
but all I see are things that I don't understand.
I conclude that I am a lousy mechanic.
Once, when I took the poem out for a spin,
down a country road overhung with the branches
of blooming trees, the sun was winking
in and out of shadow and the music was just right
and her house seemed closer, the woman who
is mostly dreamstuff. It was then that
I decided the poem was worth keeping despite any
trouble which may come later from
my lack of understanding, from my blind ignorance.
I remember how smooth the road seemed,
as if I were gliding, as if movement was all I needed,
really, to feel alive, and sharp, and loveable.

I Have Terrible Mornings

From dark to light
and I shake
like a barber. There
is a misalignment
in me that the dawn
triggers. I say to
the terror: wait. Give
me passage to noon.
I make small prayers
to infinite gods, too
tired of the petty
ways of man, too in-
terested in things
other than mornings
of dread and misalignment.
And I burn effigies of myself.
And I burn hours like chaff.
And I wake to sleep to wake.

Dorothy Parker

Dorothy Parker, wit and friend,
Met an ignominious end.
Marked her grave, Excuse my dust.
Her lovely frame grew tough with crust.

She lived to make sweet apercus.
Among the swells and New York News.
She thought that life was full of shit.
Dorothy Parker, friend and wit.

And—

The way I carry myself.
The ship on the horizon.
The pain in my thigh.
The aroma she left on the coverlet.
The matchbox car I had when I was ten.
The cuts in her cheeks.
The first poem I wrote.
The paper I kept in a bottom drawer.
The curvilinear cooling towers.
The late night talks.
The war in Vietnam.
The sadness in my mother's soul.
The calm suffering of my father.
The asthma I had undiagnosed.
The way I could hit a tennis ball.
The way I could shoot a gun.
The love, the way I could love.
The pain in my chest.
The sway of her lower back.
The news about the President.
The first adult book I read.
The first woman I saw naked.
The trips we took to Ontario.
The way I used to think.
The friends who have abandoned me.
The way I thought about friendship.
The aroma she left in my head.
The pain between my legs.
The news of my brother's cancer.
The mistake that led to pregnancy.
The shining son that came.
The first poem I wrote.
The way I feel today.
The pain in my thigh.

The love that does not die.
The love that is like pain.
The wife I will always have.
The daughter we made.
The pain in my head.
The pain that is fear.
The pain that is my absence.
The pain that is always always always.
The way you look at me when I hurt.

Beast

My senses awaken if not my sense.
Her face is beatific
if there are still believers.
She's young, as new as sinless Eden.
And she carries that
dangerousness like a sweet
pocket of powder.
I am moth, sleeper, reprobate.
My cage door swings open on its own.
I close it, as if I loved
my captors.
As if living here was what I had in mind
all the time.

O for a Muse of Fire

I dip my pin in blood,
reply to your indifference
with irony, make a
small black mark
and expect it to face things
for me. Poor
sanguinary scrivener, who would
prefer not, but who
has to. Out of love.

We've Got Life

We've got a dog.
We keep her
in the backyard.
We've got a TV.
We watch it
most nights.
We've got prescriptions.
We take them
when we are lonely
or cold or
looking for answers
We've got weather.
We use it sometimes,
as an excuse to do
something, or not.

Bruegel

Pieter Bruegel, phantom,
painter of grotesqueries,
so little we know of you,
here hundreds of years later.
We have a mania, I may
as well tell you, for biography,
for knowing the man behind
the curtain. Surely, your
hunters are enough, your
dancers, your peasants, your
everyday wonders. And, yet,
looking at something as
magisterial as *Children's Games*
or *The Fall of Icarus* one
wants to know the eyes
which first saw such grivoiserie,
and was able to secure it
for all time, on pieces of
lumber. Who *were* you?
Just another of God's angels
put among the blind like
a poor parable, like a makeshift
saint, to be studied in dens
and libraries down through time.
Just another drunken magus,
friend of Auden and Williams.

Huldre Vigilate

"The devil is hungry."
Laura Nyro

Here's a little poem about television.
There are some good things on
television. I watch them.
At night when we're alone, the two
of us, I eat a cold meal of bone
and heartmeat. The TV watches me,
for further signs of too much life.
The next day it makes me write this.

Ministration

Fingernail clippings like
slices of moon
litter the ground near my feet.
Personal discipline is
the watchword here.
My hair, a little rough at the
edges, begins to bother
me. I invite the executioner in
with a smile. I'm prone to
over-reaction, I've been warned.
The sky is overcast;
I'll wear a dark suit, the one with
creases as sharp as teeth.

The Wolf Again

> *"There are nights when the wolves are silent and only the moon howls."* -George Carlin

When the wolf
sat at the table
most of us tried to act
as if we weren't
ruffled. After
all we had eaten to-
gether before,
just never at home.
Later, when
they gave out the
prizes and the wolf
won most of what
we coveted we
still simpered. It was
only when the
women began hang-
ing around the
den, the juice on
their thighs
glistening like smiles,
did we begin to
think that what we
had ceded was
lost forever. We stopped
shaving and
began to prepare
for a journey,
one that would take
us outside the city,
to places where

we would all be foreigners,
fierce strangers at
every banquet.

Ring-a-Lievio

Line them all up
and set them
on fire.
Let the bodies fall
where bodies
fall. Let the other
team collect
whom they can.
An eye for an eye,
a tooth for
a mouthful. Your
child for mine.
The pieces left over
will be used
to build new players.
The new players
will all be fireproof.
There will be
new ways to destroy them.

The Medicine Bottle

The medicine bottle
on the counter
is a counter,
a register of things
forgettable.
You go there expecting
comfort, the
kind of friend you can
call at midnight
and say futilitarian
to. The medicine bottle
is a mouth
cursing you, loving you,
a mouth
like your last, best
lover. The one who would
take you in,
swallow you, and
wrap you in deadly daydreams.

The Idea

That the body is used up.
That it will not carry me around.
That there is a foul misalignment.
That it will not be loved again.
That it will not love again.
That you will find it wanting.
That it wants.
That I fear the next step, and the next.
That this pain is the penultimate pain if not worse.
That I have given my all.
That my all is over.
That it was not enough.
That you do not love it.
That I do not love it.
That poems have no power.
That poems have no power.
That death will come with the face of Robert Redford.
That death will be kind in the handing over.
That the preliminaries will not undo me.
That, if undone, you will remember only that I loved you.
That I loved you with everything I had.
That I loved you with these words, this idea, and oh this body.

I used to be a king

I used to be a king
and my kingdom
was a circle
and my queen was the
key, the only way out.

Dog

Saskia works like a dog,
often pulling
the late shift at the
squirrel watch.
In the gloaming she
appears a black and
white wraith, circling the
tree of knowledge,
barking at her God,
working harder
than the most ardent prayer.

Let's Do This

Let's say our best desires are
the ones that involve others.
Let's say we really believe that
connection is next to godliness.
Let's throw a party and invite those
people who insult us, who are so
edgy they have no middle. Let's
say we all dance till midnight and
when the day turns we all go back
to the animals we were meant to be.
Now let's put a sun high in the
sky and let's say its warmth is
restoration. Let's all assume we're
in this together, making it up as we
go along, singing the old songs, be-
lieving in the newest and best revolutions.

Meditation on a Thurible

The sun burns my joss stick.
I'm incensed.
The light outside is the color
of an old nickel.
From where I sit the sidewalk goes around

the world.

My bird

I had a bird once
could sing like
Jack Bruce. I called
him Bobby after the,
you know, seventh
assassination. This
bird made me happy
some mornings,
happier than you
ever did, though I love
you like a stare.
Bobby asks that I be a
singer now. This next
song is gonna kill.
Seriously, it will kill.

Little One

Inside Marda Little One
waits like an apostrophe.
It's dark and warm.
Little One cocks a partial
ear toward the wall.
The voices are full of
poetry. In the perpetual
night Little One thinks
about life and light. It's
one thing to be potential,
and another to be timeless.

CONTRANYMS

> *"All things had opposites close by, every decision a reason against it, every animal an animal that destroys it."*
> *--Patricia Highsmith*

Salad Days

1. *a period of inexperience*
2. *a heyday*

When I have lost everything
I will wait for you. You
can come by the back gate.
We will act as if we were
that couple again, the ones
who wrote the songs the
stars sing, the ones in bed
alive like children about to
set foot on freshly paved roads.

Depthless

1. *immeasurably deep*
2. *shallow*

You know that when I say
the things you count on
hearing I am twofaced. I
am the man with a soul so thick
it bleeds poems. I am the one
with thinning hair, whose
lines dry up like lies, whose
lines are rehearsed beyond sense.

Grog

    1. *a diluted alcoholic drink*
    2. *a strong alcoholic drink*

Fix me again that ptisan which
will turn me into swine. Make
it strong enough to knock the
poet out of me. Water it down
so that I may return from the sty,
a dabbler, a traveler, weak as teas.

Sententious

    1. *Full of pithy expressions.*
    2. *Full of pompous moralizing.*

I cannot wake to the challenge. I know
without the right words that I will
lose you to the dawn. I do not sleep
because the words come out in dribs,
drab as cliché, full of the wind that will
carry you from me, the wind that will
return and return, empty, silvery, bloody, vain.

Dabster

   1. *an expert*
   2. *a dabbler*

In the bedroom of frost
I wrote the lines that took
me out of myself. I woke
up a poet. I woke up a
drunkard. Only you know
my real name. I whisper
it to you when I am at my
best, when I have lost everything.

A.M.

At the edge of thought
a near-thought.
This morning the sun is
late: winter.

Acknowledgements

5 2 One: "Bitter my tongue," "And Sleep," "I think of you in poems," "In attitudes of love"
Aerings: "In my Library," "The Edge of You"
Anastomoo: "A is Easy"
Antinarrative: "My World and Welcome to It"
August Cutter: "Torn," "Sneak Thief"
Autumn Sky: "Chiasmatype"
Blood Sugar Poetry: "A barefoot woman"
Blue House: "LSD," "Ring-a-Lievio," "The Medicine Bottle"
Boston Poetry Magazine: "I Have Terrible Mornings"
Caldron: "And--," "Beast," "O for a Muse of a Fire," "A.M."
Catalonian Review: "Four Poems"
Change Seven: "Starting with my Penis"
Cherry Blossom Review: "I Go Out, I Expect Things," "Once the Poem Ran like a Dream"
Concelebratory Shoehorn Review: "We've Got Life"
Counterexample Poetics: "Distortion"
Dead Mule: "Ophelia," "Asterisk"
Ducts: "Meditation on a Thurible,"
Heavy Bear: "And the Snow Covered Everything"
Isacoustic: "Dapping for Meaning" "Dog"
Margarine Maypole Orangutan Express: "Mensuration"
Meat for Tea: "In Jackson, Mississippi," "Home in the City"
Moonwort Review: Dorothy Parker
Mystic Prophet: "Ministration"
Nixes Mate Review: "The World's Fattest Man," "I used to be a king," "The Ghost-Me"
Nude Bruce Review: "Young and Hot"
Old Hickory Review: "Meridiem"
Peacock Journal: ""Just a Little," "In Double Indemnity," "Eucalyptus, I Calyptus, We all Calyptus," "Night Voyage"
Peeking Cat: "Bosch"
Penn Review: "Third Poem"
Poetry Repairs: "Gloria Graham Grays"
Post--: "Contranyms"
Rat's Ass Review: "After the Vandals Sacked Rome," "Father, Son"
Right Hand Pointing: "Woodpecker," "Here"

Ristau Journal: "Let's Do This" "I can't fix it either"
Rockvale Review: "The Dark Clock"
Saucy Vox: "Bruegel"
Shadowtrain: "The Word Would be Go"
Slant: "Gathering, Disruption"
South Florida Poetry Journal: "Kool like Klaus Kinski"
Subterranean Blue: "A murmuration of starlings"
Telegraph: Seeing the Pill Clearly
The Courtship of Winds: "I Never Saw my Father Drunk"
The Legendary: "Chekhov," "Inside Again," "The Dog's Song"
Triplopia: "The Recovery"
Void: "The Wolf Again"
Whimperbang: "The Best Cowboy"
Ygdrasil: "Huldre Vigilate"

photo credit: Sandra Smith-McDougall

COREY MESLER has been published in numerous anthologies and journals including *Poetry, Gargoyle, Five Points, Good Poems American Places,* and *New Stories from the South*. He has published nine novels, four short story collections, and five full-length poetry collections, and a dozen chapbooks. His novel, *Memphis Movie*, attracted kind words from Ann Beattie, Peter Coyote, and William Hjorstberg, among others. He's been nominated for the Pushcart many times, and three of his poems were chosen for Garrison Keillor's Writer's Almanac. He also wrote the screenplay for *We Go On*, which won The Memphis Film Prize in 2017. With his wife he runs a 143 year-old bookstore in Memphis. He can be found at https://coreymesler.wordpress.com.

Made in the USA
Columbia, SC
20 August 2018